Ant & Dec

Andy Croft

Published in association with The Basic Skills Agency

Hodder Murray

A MEMBER OF THE HODDER HEADLINE GROUP

The Publishers would like to thank the following for permission to reproduce copyright material:

Photo credits
p.2 © Mark Campbell/Rex Features; p.6 © STB/Rex Features; p.9 © Action Press/Rex Features; p.13 © Peter Jordan/PA Photos; p.16 Ken McKay/Rex Features; p.18 © All Action Pictures Ltd.; p.23 KMK/LWT/Rex Features.

Orders: please contact Bookpoint Ltd, 130 Milton Park, Abingdon, Oxon OX14 4SB. Telephone (44) 01235 827720. Fax: (44) 01235 400454. Lines are open from 9.00–6.00, Monday to Saturday, with a 24-hour message answering service. You can also order through our website www.hoddereducation.co.uk

Copyright © Andy Croft 2003, 2005
Second Edition. First published in 2003 by
Hodder Murray, a member of the Hodder Headline Group
338 Euston Road
London NW1 3BH

Impression number 10 9 8 7 6 5 4 3 2 1
Year   2010 2009 2008 2007 2006 2005

Cover photo © Ken McKay/Rex Features
Typeset in 14pt Palatino by SX Composing DTP, Rayleigh, Essex.
Printed in Great Britain by CPI Bath.

A catalogue record for this title is available from the British Library

ISBN-10 0 340 90075 X
ISBN-13 978 0 340 90075 8

Contents

1 Who Are They ?

They are actors.
They are pop stars.
They are comedians.
They are TV presenters.

They sound funny.
They look funny.
They are funny.

They are famous.
They have won lots of awards.
They are always on TV.
They are two of the most popular entertainers
in Britain.

Who are they?

Ant and Dec.

Ant and Dec with the Celebrity Soccer Six Cup.

2 Geordie Lads

Ant was born on 18 November 1975
in Newcastle.
His real name is Anthony David McPartlin.
His Mum is called Christine.
His Dad is called Ray.
He has a sister called Sarah
and a half-sister called Emma.
They all lived in a three-bedroom house
in Fenham, Newcastle.

Dec was born on 25 September 1975
in Newcastle.
His real name is Declan Joseph Oliver Donnelly.
His Mum is called Anne.
His Dad is called Alphonsus.
They ran a pub.

He has three sisters,
called Patricia, Moira and Camelia,
and three brothers,
called Eamon, Martin and Dermot.
Dec is the youngest of seven children.
He also grew up in a three-bedroom house
in Fenham, Newcastle.

People from Newcastle
are called 'Geordies'.
Newcastle United
are called 'the Toon'.
Ant and Dec support Newcastle United.
They are members of
the Toon Army.

3 'Byker Grove'

When Dec was 13,
he saw an advert in the local paper.
It said the BBC were looking for kids
to act in a TV series set in a Newcastle youth club.
The series was called 'Byker Grove'.

Dec phoned the BBC in Newcastle.
They asked him for an audition.
Dec got the part of Duncan in 'Byker Grove'.

At the start of the second series,
Dec met a new boy.
He was playing PJ in the series.
He was sitting in the corner
with his head in his hands.
Dec thought he looked grumpy.
It was Ant.

Ant and Dec at the tenth anniversary of 'Byker Grove'.

Ant had already starred
in a daytime kids' programme
called 'Why Don't You?'

PJ and Duncan soon became best friends.
So did Ant and Dec.

'Byker Grove' was very popular.
It made Ant and Dec famous.
PJ and Duncan were always up to something.
They went on a ghost hunt.
Duncan performed a magic show.
PJ was in a charity show.
Duncan joined a strange group
called the Psychandrics.
PJ was blinded playing paintball.
Duncan stole PJ's girlfriend.

They formed a band called Grove Matrix.
When it was PJ's 17th birthday
they sang a song called 'Tonight I'm Free'.
Fans of the series wanted to buy it.
The lads signed a record contract
and the song went straight into the charts.

A few weeks later the lads left 'Byker Grove'.
They wanted to try something new.
They wanted to be pop stars.
Some people said they weren't good enough.
But they were wrong.

PJ and Duncan, 1995.

4 PJ and Duncan

After 'Tonight I'm Free',
they released 'Why Me?'
Their third single was 'Let's Get Ready to Rumble'.
It was the summer smash of 1994.
It reached number 9 in the charts.
PJ and Duncan sang the song on 'Top of the Pops'.
'If I Give You My Number' reached 15.
'Eternal Love' reached 12.

Their first album, *Psyche*,
sold over 400,000 copies.
It reached number 4 in the album charts.

They made a video
called 'Whose Video Is It Anyway?'
It reached number 2 in the UK video charts.

At the end of 1994,
they won the *Smash Hits*/Radio 1 Best New Act
award.

PJ and Duncan released 14 singles
and 3 albums.
They were going to make another album,
but they decided to retire from pop music.
They wanted to try something new.
They wanted to be TV stars.
Some people said they weren't good enough.
But they were wrong.

5 Saturday Morning TV

Ant and Dec made two series
of 'The Ant and Dec Show' for BBC1.
It was very funny.
It was very popular.
They used to ask children questions.
If a child gave the wrong answer,
Ant and Dec cut off their hair!

They made 'Ant and Dec Unzipped'
for Channel 4.

But their biggest hit was
ITV's Saturday morning show,
'SM:tv' (Saturday Morning TV).
It started in 1998
and ran for three years.
It starred Ant, Dec and Cat Deeley.
There were kids in the studio,
jokes, sketches, cartoons,
competitions and games.

Ant and Dec with Cat Deeley.

After 'SM:tv' came 'CD:UK'.
There was lots of live music,
competitions, interviews, prizes and the pop charts.
It was the most popular music show in the UK.

Ant and Dec were brilliant kids' TV presenters.
But they wanted to try something new.
They wanted to be comedians.
Some people said they weren't good enough.
But they were wrong.

6 Funny Men

Ant and Dec are now one of the funniest
comic acts on British TV.

Ant and Dec have starred in their own
Saturday night TV shows:
'Friends Like These',
'Slap Bang',
'Saturday Night Takeaway'.

'Saturday Night Takeaway'
was a game show.
The winner took home
prizes from last week's adverts.
Sometimes it was a new car.
Sometimes it was a packet of biscuits!

'Ant and Dec's Saturday Night Takeaway'.

They made a TV comedy set in Newcastle
called 'The Likely Lads'.

Ant and Dec have starred in a Christmas pantomime,
'Snow White and the Seven Dwarfs'.
They have presented 'The Big Breakfast'.
They have presented the *Smash Hits* party.
They have presented the Brit Awards.
They have presented the Record of the Year
Awards.
They have presented Comic Relief.
They have hosted the National Lottery draw.
They have presented 'Pop Idol'.
They have presented 'I'm a Celebrity,
Get Me Out of Here'.

Ant and Dec have made TV adverts
for Cadbury's chocolate, McDonald's and
Woolworths.

In 2000, they returned to 'Byker Grove'
as PJ and Duncan.

Ant and Dec with Will Young and Gareth Gates at the
final of 'Pop Idol' in 2002.

In 2002, they wrote a song for the World Cup,
'On The Ball'.
It was the official England World Cup song.
They sang it on 'Top of the Pops'.

There are wax models of Ant and Dec
at Madame Tussaud's in London.

In 2002, they won three prizes
at the National Television Awards in London.
They were voted Top Entertainers
for the second year running.
Their show 'Pop Idol' was voted
the Most Popular Entertainment Programme.
They were also given a Special Recognition Award
for all their work on TV.
When they were given the award,
Dec said, 'We really are speechless.
We haven't got a speech!'

Ant and Dec are the voices
for a new pre-school cartoon called 'Engie Benjy'.
Dec is the voice behind Engie Benjy.
Ant plays a dog called Jollop.

What will they try next?
It could be anything!

7 Ant and Dec Fact File

Ant

Height:	5 ft 8in.
Star sign:	Scorpio.
Favourite colour:	Blue.
Favourite book:	*The Beach* by Alex Garland.
Favourite film:	*The Thin Red Line.*
Nicknames:	Forehead, Smiler.
Hates:	Spiders, Sunderland FC.
Likes:	'The Simpsons'.

Dec

Height:	5 ft 6in.
Star sign:	Libra.
Shoe size:	6½!
Favourite colour:	Orange.
Favourite film:	*One Flew Over the Cuckoo's Nest.*
Favourite band:	Badly Drawn Boy.
Hates:	Cats.

8 Just Like Twins

Everyone knows Ant and Dec.
But not everyone knows
which is Ant and which is Dec.
If you are not sure,
Ant is always on the left,
and Dec is always on the right.

Some people think they are twins.
They both have cheeky smiles.
They share the same silly sense of humour.
They are both small.

They were born a few weeks apart.
They both grew up in a three-bedroom house
in the same part of Newcastle.
They both support Newcastle United.

Ant and Dec with Jordan and Kerry McFadden on 'I'm a Celebrity Get Me Out of Here' in 2004.

When Ant was a baby he broke his arm.
He had to have a metal pin put in.
He still has a scar on his elbow
from the operation.
Ant is scared of spiders.
Ant sometimes sleeps
in a Newcastle United shirt!

Dec's favourite hobby is watching football.
When he was six, he fell off his bike
and bit through his tongue.
He broke his nose playing football
on the set of 'Byker Grove'.

When Ant was caught speeding,
he was banned from driving for three months.
So Dec had to drive him everywhere.

Ant and Dec used to share a flat in London.
Now they live in separate houses.
Next door to each other!
Each house is worth £800,000.

9 TV Series Starring Ant and Dec

'Byker Grove'	1989/90–3
'The Ant and Dec Show'	1995–6
'Ant and Dec'	1996–7
'Ant and Dec Unzipped'	1997
'The Big Breakfast'	1998
'SM:tv'	1998–2001
'CD:UK'	1998–2001

'Ant and Dec's Secret Camera Show'	2000
'Friends Like These'	2000–1
'Slap Bang'	2001
'Pop Idol'	2001–3
'I'm a Celebrity, Get me Out of Here'	2002–5
'Saturday Night Takeaway'	2002–5
'The Likely Lads'	2004